Muhzina S.

Invincible Publishers

First published in India in 2019

ISBN : 978-93-88333-50-4

Invincible Publishers

201A, SAS Tower, Sector 38, Gurgaon-122003

Registered Address: Opposite Kasturba Ashram,
Radaur, Haryana–135133

Printed at Thomson Press (India) LTD

This is a work of fiction. Any names or characters, businesses or places, events or incidents, are fictitious. Any resemblance to actual persons, living or dead, or actual events is purely coincidental.

To my dear grandpa Jamaludheen Kunju, who was a wonderful human being and who stood by people in their times of need.

To all the brave people who fight against the injustices prevailing in the society.

Acknowledgement

My sincere thanks to the following people who have helped me in this journey of writing:

All those wonderful women who are not ready to give up despite the hardships faced by them, who gave me the inspiration to write this novel.

Anjali Anil, my friend and first reader who encouraged me to proceed further in writing.

Aneesha Mathew P, my bestie who like a mirror, corrects me and spread her wild ideas into me.

Steny P S, for being my Steny Jacob.

Mery Dincy, Katharin John, Ancy Anthony, and Amrutha Udayakumar – my gang who will be with me in all my madness.

All my friends from **Canossa Hostel** and **St Joseph's College** who encouraged me in writing.

All my buddies of the one and only **XII B**.

All my teachers and sisters of **Mary Mount Public School** and **St Joseph's College**.

My family and relatives, for provoking me everytime.

My publishers, for making my dream come true.

And finally,you reader, for giving my book a chance.

Preface

All of us have heard the statement, "A pen is mightier than a sword." Many writers use their pens to fight against the injustices prevailing in the society. Well, recent attacks on people expressing their views and ideas, either through writing or any other media proves that their words have reached the aimed point.

As a matter of fact, my anger is the one thing that droveme into writing.There are many things that would have gone right if we didn't shut our eyes because of our laziness. Waiting for others to do our job will keep us waiting for years. Through this work, I intend to show that there are people who listen to their heart and show courage to do the right thing.

This work is a tribute to all the great journalists and activists all over the world who stand for the truth and the upliftment of the underprivileged. Their voice has helped a lot in such times when those in power failed to remember what the ordinary people wanted. Hats off to them!

I tried to provide you readers the confusions and hardships that one has to face when they try to follow what our societynow calls as an utopian idea – 'Following what our heart says.'

Life won't be easy. If it is easy, then it is not life. Many fail to rise after each fall. Failures may come and go. But the real failure is not rising from your fall and keep complaining about it.

Here I present the story of some people who are not ready to give up.

Happy reading.

CHAPTER 1

It was a ghastly morning. Well, one can't call it a morning! The sky was all filled up with coal black cloud. It reminded her of black currant.

She was on her journey to Kuttikanam, a high range Village in Idukki. Yes, it was indeed a long journey, an inter-state one, to be specific. Yet, she was very much excited. The three-day journey which started from Karnataka didn't seem to cast a tint of tiredness in her.

Shivangi Manohar. Twenty-one years old. Half Kannadiga, half-Malayali. "What a lovely girl" people would say on seeing her. As active as an ant, when social service plunged its roots deep into her head, she joined BSW.

Students have to present a project work during the last year of their degree course. Shivangi thought and thought. Finally, she remembered her journey to Idukki when she was about twelve. It was the neighbouring district of her father's family. Such a beautiful place it was. Then she thought about poor tea plantation workers whom she met there.

"Yes... this is it! My project will be on the lives of those people." And that's how she choose Kuttikkanam and this journey.

Shivangi's papa Mr Manohar Raj is a businessman. His family is settled in Eranakulam, district next to Idukki. He was the eldest of three sons of Mr and Mrs Rajendhran Nair. Manohar was so hardworking that after his few years in the business world, he made a successful platform for himself. His family was so proud of him and that is why they didn't oppose when Manohar thought of marrying Sulatha, a pure Kannadiga girl whom he met in one of his business trips.

Their marriage was a grand ceremony and after three years, Shivangi was born. Their only daughter, she was the one who came to this world after a lot of prayers by her parents and relatives. Sulatha never thought she can give birth to a child as she was having some problem in her uterus. But she craved for one very badly. God had heard her and blessed the couple with Shivangi. Because of this, they never let her down for anything. They would die to satisfy and complete her wishes. But she never made use of this situation. What a sweet girl!

Manohar, along with Sulatha and Shivangi, moved to Karnataka when Shivangi was five years old. He thought of focussing his business in Karnataka. Sulatha was very happy too. Rajendran and Indira were sad as they could no longer play with their grandchild, yet they believed it is for their son's better future. They visited them every summer vacation and made them happy.

It was Divakar's idea of Shivangi staying in his estate for the time she was at Kuttikanam. Divakar Raj is the younger brother of Manohar. Shivangi's uncle. He followed the path of his brother and became a businessman. He bought an estate in Kuttikanam for he thought that it might be of some use someday. And now, it was useful for Shivangi!

By the time she reached the estate, it was raining black and blue. She had never seen such a heavy rain before. She feared whether it is a bad omen or not, since she was indeed a very religious girl. Sulatha had brought her up so.

Chinnamma, the main servant of the estate was waiting for her at the gate. She was a thin woman of fifty.

"Come inside Mol, is there any problem for me to call you 'Mol'?" she asked.

Shivangi knew that it means 'daughter'. Her grandparents frequently call her so.

"No problem, Chinnamma you can call me Mol."

The estate was really big one. It reminded her of the larger estates that she had seen in horror movies. She thought and could never find a fine reason to stay all alone in that estate. But Chinnamma promised that she would be there all the time. Besides, her project partner will come after a couple of days. So, she decided to stay in the estate.

CHAPTER 2

Idukki is a high range district. Astonishingly magical! The one that could make any tourist spellbound.

Shivangi was also fascinated, but the hair-pin roads made her empty the stomach. It was the only problem she faced during the journey.

Kuttikanam is really a visual paradise. It is 3500 feet above the sea level. It is surrounded by lush of green tea plantations. Mundakayam and Kanjirappally are the two neighbouring towns. It is within the territory of Peermade, another famous tourist spot.

Chinnamma introduced her to some people, waiting by the gate, all of them the native working class of Kuttikanam tea plantation. Shivangi behaved as nicely as she could and talked to them in such a way that she made an impact on them even at their first meeting. She was careful not to hurt them with her words. After all, it was their response that would strengthen her project. So it was important for her to keep them happy with her interaction.

There were six of them – Kannan, his wife Muthamma, Johnny, Pappy, Radha, and her husband Gopi. Kannan was the watchman cum manager of the estate. Divakar met him when he was in Kuttikanam and after knowing him, he gave him the task of looking after the estate. Divakar himself certified him as the best manager the estate could have! Through Kannan, almost all of the plantation workers came to know about Shivangi's arrival.

After her conversation with them, Chinnamma led her into the estate. The front door was twice that of which was at her home. She thought of the need for such a big door. She calmed herself by saying that it will suit the big estate anyway.

She put her luggage into one room Chinnamma had shown her. It was quite a big room. She was so curious to explore the estate that she postponed even freshening up.

She went to the front porch. The surrounding beauty made her stupefied. It was very scenic. The estate was surrounded by green, green and green only. She feared that she would forget all other work and would only enjoy the beauty of this place!

After spending about an hour outside, she returned to freshen up. That is when she noticed something in the main hall. She had never paid attention to it when she arrived in the estate. It was the framed photo of a young and beautiful lady.

"Chinnamma , can you please come here?"

"Yes, Mol I'm coming" she came in a swish.

"Whose photo is this?" asked Shivangi pointing to it.

"This was the daughter of the former owner of this estate."

"'Was' the daughter?" Shivangi got confused.

"Yes Mol, 'was' the daughter. She died few months back. You don't worry. I will remove the photo now."

"No, no it's ok. Let it be there."

"Your wish. I am going to the kitchen. Call me if you need anything."

"Okay Chinnamma."

After she left, Shivangi turned to the photo.

"Poor thing, she might be of my age or a little older. It is inappropriate to call back people when they are so young, oh God!" she thought.

CHAPTER 3

Shivangi had a shower and decided to arrange her belongings into the cupboard. She had got her mother's sense of cleanliness and neatness. Sulatha never postponed her cleaning mission of the house at any time, and so did Shivangi.

She started unpacking and put them neatly in the cupboard. Then she noticed a paper lying in it. It was a handwritten note.

"VIRANGANA – WHO'S SHE?"

- *Jessica Mathew*

"Girls should not be allowed to travel alone at late times."

We have been hearing this stigmatic sentence for a long time. People have been saying this since time immemorial and now, it continues. I would like to start by quoting a question from the Malayalam movie 'Queen'.

"Which is the so-called 'late time' for a woman that is not at all applicable for a man?"

As seen in recent incidents, girls are often blamed for any misconduct happening to them. They have to bear it along with the physical torture that they faced. Why is it happening? Why is there always a loop hole for the guilty rapists? Why the prey (I hate to use that word, no woman is a deer whom the lion feeds) is left with no options and forced to keep quiet? Why the courts have made sensible verdicts, going silly behind evidences and totally neglecting what the victim had to face? Even if the convict is sent to a prison, are the internal conditions appropriate to make him feel remorseful for his deed?

Ours is considered to be a patriarchal society. Okay, there is nothing to 'consider'. Ours is truly a patriarchal society, no one can deny it. I am not a feminist, I can assure you that. But it's hard not to mention that this patriarchy has made the lives of a million women in darkness. We have heard of the suppression faced by Namboothiri women in Kerala during earlier times. Even though time has changed, the suppression did not end. It only changed its form, to a more elite level!

A woman fears to disclose her trouble to the society because of the rude comments she has to face from the people. I watch in wonder how defenders rise among the public in favour of the guilty person! How can they just stamp upon a woman who has already been downtrodden by heartless criminals?

I just wanted to ask these defenders a question. What will you say if your daughter is raped by someone? Will you support and shelter her or will you go and defend the convict?

Please stop seeing the victim as a total stranger. Consider her as our daughter or sister. Then you can see yourself melting away and you will support her from the bottom of your heart. Then you can't blame her for going out at the so-called 'late time'.

"Oh, it's not complete. Where are the other papers?"

Shivangi, who was now interested in the essay became irritated to find that the work is incomplete.

"That Jessica could have completed it. It was so interesting! But who on earth is Jessica and why is this paper here?"

CHAPTER 4

She kept the paper aside and continued unpacking. There were not much clothes. She took all her books for reference which constituted three-fourth of the luggage. Three weeks were allowed for the project work. Christmas vacation would commence then. Three plus two, five weeks. She will get five weeks for her project.

She arranged the books in the lower shelf. Everything was neat and clean.

She turned to the bed and found an album lying in the bed. Might have fallen down when she took the books in bulk. She called it 'Memory House'. It was indeed a memory house. She got all special moments captured and gathered it in the album.

She flipped the pages one by one. The first picture was that of her first birthday celebration, Manohar and Sulatha kissing the baby Shivangi.

The album also contained her each birthday celebrations, her dance performances, she smiling proudly and holding her best student award, and so on.

Suddenly she blushed on seeing a photo. Her cheeks turned pinkish-red and couldn't hide smile. It was Pulkit's picture.

Pulkit is in her college—same batch, same class. His house is just opposite to that of her. He is in the music club with her; he is in the tennis club with her. It's like 'Wherever you go, I am there' style. He will be with her all the time. Naturally, this was enough for them to fall in love.

Pulkit Modi was a full-on Gujarathi settled in Bangalore. His father Anurag Modi is a businessman, just like Manohar. Pulkit and Shivangi were classmates from sixth standard onwards. They were good friends till twelfth standard. But when they entered the college, everything changed.

Pulkit was a sensation in the college, pakka Varun Dhawan type. Girls were running behind him. They thrived to get a glance from him. But he never minded them. It was like he was not even interested in them.

Many of the friends advised him to make the girls happy and take one or two for a date, but he never fell for them. It was abnormal for a boy of this age to avoid a bunch of girls who are mad after him. So his friends kept questioning him. Finally, it fell out of his mouth. He loved Shivangi for a long time and still loves her. He never disclosed it to her, on the fear that she might not take it in a good way and will never even talk to him after.

But his friends... they made him tell her the truth. They black mailed him by saying that if he never disclosed to her about his love, they would paint it on the college wall! He agreed to tell her.

It was their college's Arts Day. Shivangi was arranging the chairs in the auditorium. All others had gone for their lunch. Pulkit approached her slowly.

"Hi Shivangi."

"Hey Pulkit, why are you just standing there? Come and help me."

"Oh yes, Shivangi…"

"What? You can't help?"

"No it's not that..."

"Then what?"

"I want to tell you something."

"Go on, why are you shivering Pulkit? Are you okay?"

"Yeah, I'm good."

"And?"

"I.... I....."

"You?"

"I love you," he said in a gulp.

"I know that!" she said suddenly.

"You? What? How?" his eyes popped out as if he had seen a big foot.

"I am not dumb to never notice your behaviour towards me. When you talk, your eyes tell you love me, your smile tells you love me."

"And what about you?" he asked.

"What about me?"

"Why didn't you confess your love to me, Shivangi?"

"That's because... wait, when did I tell I love you?"

He didn't reply. Instead he came close to her. He looked into her eyes. After a minute, he spoke.

"I never had the strength to identify this before, Shivangi; your eyes say you love me. And I was so stupid not to notice it before."

She didn't say a word, she just hugged him!

When Manohar and Sulatha got to know about this, they never stormed out. They were happy for her. They knew Pulkit very well. They believed she couldn't get another boy who is as nice as him. They were all happy. This was also the case with Anurag Modi and his wife Rani Modi.

Sometimes Manohar mocked by saying that their house is a living proof of India's cultural heritage, with people from three different states!

Pulkit now went to Bihar for his project, but he promised to call her every day.

Shivangi felt weary after unpacking, so she decided to get some sleep.

CHAPTER 5

"Kuttikanam was under the rule of Changanassery kings during 16th century and was uninhabited. In 1756, this place was brought under the supremacy of the King of Travancore. A church society missionary, Henry Baker started coffee plantations in Kuttikanam and under the regency of Sree Moolam Thirunal, these became tea plantations.

Under the British Raj in India, Kuttikanam became an up-market resort. The summer palace of Travancore kings was shifted to Kuttikanam. During the British periods and after, manpower was brought to this place from various parts of Kerala and Tamil Nadu. The descendants of these migrant workers constitute a major part of the population of Kuttikanam."

The history of Kuttikanam was explained to Shivangi by Vinayachandran. He was a retired school teacher, people used to call him 'Vinayan Mash' which means 'Teacher Vinayan'. He used his leisure time to spread the knowledge about Kuttikanam to the tourists. Shivangi met him on her evening walk. After knowing her purpose of arrival, he promised her that he would help her in all possible ways. He asked her to approach him when needed.

Shivangi was multilingual and knew six languages – Kannada, Malayalam, Hindi, Tamil, English, and French. Knowing Malayalam and Tamil made her conversation with the natives much easier. Even though Idukki is a district of Kerala, there were many migrants from Tamil

Nadu in the tea plantations of Kuttikanam who knew no other language than Tamil.

Shivangi walked past the plantations and saw many women collecting the tea leaves. Their experience had made them work in a fast pace.

She moved forward and found a bunch of children playing Kuttiyum Kolum. They invited her to play with them and she accepted it. They taught her how to play Kuttiyum Kolum and found it very interesting. She spent some time with them. She even invited the kids to the estate and promised them chocolates she bought from Bangalore.

"You are so nice, chechi," one of them said.

"But not as nice as you guys," she replied.

The children giggled. They promised to visit the estate and she continued her walk.

CHAPTER 6

Shivangi decided to start her project survey from the very next day. At first, she pondered to wait for her project partner. But she decided to get started.

She woke up at six in the morning. After a short session of exercise, she came for breakfast. Chinnamma had prepared appam and fish molly for her. She had tried it before when she came to Ernakulam for visiting her grandparents. Sulatha, even though a good cook, knew little about Kerala delicacies. Manohar had no special demands for food and would eat whatever Sulatha had prepared. So was Shivangi.

After her breakfast, she set out to meet Mr. Naran Kanthan. He was Divakar's friend and owned a tea factory. He allowed her to take a look at the factory procedures and working of people and machinery. She found that labours had no special duties inside the factory; machineries performed most of the work. The main need for manpower was in the cultivation of tea leaves and in the packing sector.

Naran informed that usually plantation owners don't allow people from outside to conduct any forms of survey on the workers without their knowledge. They feared that if they wake the rebels in their minds, who are kept silent nowadays, it could lead to a clash between the workers and owners. And it had happened before many a times. He made her promise that she would only ask about their life style and working conditions and never discuss anything else. He also asked her not to disturb them during their working hours. She agreed.

She got out from the factory and then suddenly hit a girl. She might be fifteen or sixteen. A thin, tall one.

"Ayyo!" she cried.

"I'm sorry. I didn't see you coming. Are you alright?" Shivangi asked.

"Yes, chechi. Are you a tourist?"

"Well, sort of. I came here for a study—a project work."

"Oh, so you are Shivangi. Divakar sir's niece!"

"Wow! You know me."

"Kannan uncle told us about you," she said.

"Really? What is your name?"

"I am Ammu. My mother works here. I came to give her the lunch."

"Lunch?"

"Yes, chechi. She will leave the house very early in the morning. So, she can't prepare anything. I will make the breakfast and lunch and will bring it to her."

"It must be hard for you to manage between house and school."

"Yes, it is. That is why I left the school," Ammu said with a sigh.

"You left it?"

"Yes, I have four younger siblings. If I go to school, there will be no one to look after them. Besides, school means a lot more expenditure. My father left us and Amma is trying hard to make ends meet. So I decided to quit the school."

Shivangi had no words for her. She tried to console her, but couldn't do it.

"I am so sorry, Ammu."

"Don't be sorry. This is not just my story. All of us are living in utter poverty. You will come to know about them slowly."

After promising to meet again, Ammu left. Shivangi stood there with a heavy heart.

CHAPTER 7

The first day of work filled her mind with sorrow. She met few women like Ammu, but older. They shared similar stories.

Shantha, who was forty-three, had to look after her paralysed husband and three children. Her wages were meagre, which was nothing to buy her husband a day's medicine. She was illiterate. She wanted her kids to study, but could not help them. Some NGO people had taught them the alphabets and few nursery rhymes, and that was all what they got.

Bhanu, fifty-two, had a badly built house. One could not call it a house, it was rather a shed! It leaked badly during rainy season and was also the home of many reptiles. She herself was an asthma patient which made her work horrible during the misty mornings. Her husband worked as a watchman. They didn't have a child. Bhanu was sad about that, but thanked God for not sending a life to this hell! Yes, she said, hell it was. No proper food, no proper living conditions…

Shivangi realised the need to make her mind little stronger. Lest she could not survive here a week by hearing their heart-sinking stories.

Ting…… Ting …… Ting …..

She was awakened from her thoughts by the door bell.

"Look Shivi mol, see who all have come to see you," Chinnamma called.

She went to the front door and was surprised to see the same kids with whom she played Kuttiyum Kolum. She never thought they would come to her.

She called them inside and Chinnamma served them lemon juice. Shivangi gave them the chocolates she had promised. They were excited and happy on seeing the chocolates.

"Chechi, why this one is white in colour? Chocolates are brown, right?" asked one.

"This one is called white chocolate," she replied.

"Mmm…it's tasty," said another kid and everyone agreed.

They played for an hour with her and left. Within that hour, the kids had taught her a handful of new games that she had never played before. Shivangi became a girl of ten before them. She played her heart out with those children. Chinnamma watched her with a smile.

After the kids left, she felt an emptiness. She called her mother and cried for some time. Sulatha was frightened by her behaviour. But as Shivangi explained her meeting with the ladies and their sad stories, Sulatha felt pleased by the pure and innocent mind of her daughter. She asked her to worry and pray to God when she was in sorrow.

Manohar was busy and didn't accept the call. She knew about his schedule, so she didn't feel cross with him.

Then she called Pulkit. He was on his way to the hotel where he stayed.

"What happened to your voice? You cried, right?" he asked.

"No."

"You are lying, Shivangi. I can sense even a slight variation in your voice. Now tell me, what is the matter?

"I was just thinking about their lives, the workers in the plantations."

"That's all?"

"Yeah."

"You are not worried about me? I thought you cried because you miss me!"

"Oh Pulkit, shut up."

"I was kidding," he laughed.

"How's your project going?" she asked.

"Good. Going well. Living conditions are bad in the street where I am working. I wonder why the authorities are not even providing them free necessary items. They could have given at least half the attention that they pay towards tourism and other celebrations."

"Oh, I think my boy is on fire!" she giggled.

"That's right. Well, don't stress out Shivangi. It is not good for your health."

"Okay, okay"

"Good. I will call you tomorrow. Love you."

"Love you too."

CHAPTER 8

Next morning, Shivangi woke up a little late. She went for the breakfast and found that Chinnamma had prepared idli, sambhar, and chutney.

Shivangi took three idlis and Chinnamma began to serve sambhar.

"No, no Chinnamma. Chutney is the combination for idli. I don't like sambhar with idli."

"Good gracious! This is exactly what Jessica Mol said," Chinnamma said with wonder.

"Jessica? You know her?"

"She is the one in the picture," she said as she pointed to the photo in the main hall.

Chinnamma continued.

"Shivi Mol, you know something. You remind me of Jessica. She was just like you — active, smart, loving and caring. I watched you yesterday playing with those kids. Jessica was also very fond of children and played with them. Many of the people whom you met here have also mentioned it to me. Jessica was really a jewel, poor girl!"

"Chinnamma, how did she die? Is it because of some disease?"

"No. Jessica was a journalist and social worker. She had tried very hard to help these poor people. And that had made her surrounded with enemies. She was murdered by someone. The police are trying to find the culprit. Her body is not found yet."

"What! Then how can you be so sure that she is dead?"

"They had found her bloody belongings from where people saw her for the last time. The place was all covered with blood. The murderer must have buried the body somewhere," Chinnamma sighed and went to the kitchen.

Shivangi found the food difficult to swallow after hearing this.

"Poor Jessica. What happened to her was very bad. I hope they will catch the culprits as early as possible. It is important to provide justice to a girl who had devoted much of her time for the welfare of poor workers," Shivangi thought.

She looked at her photo. "Jessica has a beautiful smile," she said to herself.

She then lit a diya under her photo. It is a custom to lit one under the pictures of dead people. Even though Jessica was a Christian, Shivangi thought that lighting diya could bring peace to her.

Suddenly a silent breeze blew and the fire in the diya got extinguished. She again lit it, but the same thing happened again.

She became frightened and dropped the idea of lighting diya. Anyway, hers was an unnatural death. What if it is her ghost that is turning off the diya! Sometimes, situations make even the intelligent people to think stupidly!

She even called Pulkit and shared her doubt.

"Are you mad? You are living in the 21st century. Behave like one," he said.

"But..."

"No but. Nothing. Don't think unnecessary things. Focus on your project," he advised.

But she could not take Jessica out of her mind. She kept thinking about her.

In the evening during tea time, Shivangi decided to ask more about her to Chinnamma.

"Chinnamma, what else do you know about Jessica?"

"I know her from her childhood days. Her father Mathew Abraham was an architect. This estate was his father's property which came to him after his father's death. Her mother Clara was a kind and generous lady. She had a brother, David. They moved into the estate when Jessica was four. I was their servant from that time till Jessica Mol passed away," she said and wiped tears from her eyes.

"Her parents and brother, where are they now?"

"Her parents passed away in an accident few months before her death. The estate was given to Jessica in their will. But after her death, it went to David and he sold it to your uncle."

"Where is David now?"

"He is a businessman and now lives in Ernakulam. He was so broken by the death of three family members within such a short time. He didn't want to keep this estate by his own as it will remind him of his sweet sister's murder by some cruel men. So he decided to sell it," saying that, Chinnamma left.

Shivangi sat there in silence. She stood and slowly walked towards Jessica's framed photo. She took the diya and passed the fire from a lighter. After ten seconds, it went off!

CHAPTER 9

Shivangi found it difficult to control herself. "What a place is this! It has not given a little peace to me. The scenic beauty is just a consolation to the trouble one faces here. First, stories from those ladies and now Jessica! I just can't focus on my project on hearing those stories. I can't put away Jessica from my mind," she told Pulkit when he called.

She never told it to her mom and dad fearing that they might call her back.

"Shivi, why are you thinking too much? You can't do anything to make the lives of those ladies better. Our authorities have to think about it. And for Jessica too, you are helpless. She is dead and there is no point in worrying for her," he said.

"What will I do to drive her out of my mind?"

"It's silly for you to think so much of a girl whom you have never even met in your life."

"I know that Pulkit, help me now."

"Okay. Do one thing. Close your eyes and think about me! You will feel relaxed."

"Dumbo! It's not funny it's not time for your poor jokes," she roared.

"Hey hey, why are you shouting? Okay, I'm sorry I should not have told a joke now. I promise that I will never tell you a joke again!"

"Pulkit, please stop making fun of me. Anyway, I'm sorry for shouting at you," her voice softened.

"Apology accepted I will try not to mock you. Now, don't cry."

"Pulkit, can I ask you something?"

"Go on, Shivi."

"Will you come here, please I want to see you I am missing you very badly." saying that, she started sobbed.

"My girl, what happened to you? I thought you are a strong girl. You have changed in a couple of days. What's the matter? I want my old Shivangi; the cheerful, the naughty, the bold Shivangi."

"Pulkit..."

"Yeah dear I'm here, I will be with you in all your goods and bads. Tell me what is bothering you?"

"Pulkit, I'm so scared," her voice shivered.

"Scared? Why?"

"I think Jessica's ghost is wandering here and there I have tried many a times to light diya before her photo. But each time, it will go off it's not normal."

"Oh my Shivi, we have talked about it earlier. It is just the wind and not any ghosts! You should have never gone to Kuttikanam. How can I come to you without completing the project?"

"Oh, I forgot. Don't worry, complete your project first it's ok, Pulkit."

"But how can I leave you in this condition? I will come. You are more important to me than any projects."

"Dear, I will be fine."

"Then, why did you ask me to come?"

"Mood swing! Never mind I am stupid sometimes. Now you forget me and do your work. If I want to see you again, I will close my eyes..."

"...And I will be there in your heart," he completed her sentence.

"That's right Mr.Varun Dhawan, I just wanted to ask you a question I never asked before, because I forget it every time. I see many girls, most of them 'ultramodern', are mad about you. They were running behind you. But why did you choose me? I mean, they were much better than me in their looks and intellect."

"So, that is your question?"

"Yes, reply please."

"That is because Varun Dhawan will look only for Alia Bhatt, and you are my Alia."

She felt goose bumps on hearing this.

"Now, are your queries over?" he asked.

"Yes."

"I love you Shivi, and do one thing for me."

"What is it?"

"Stop thinking about Jessica."

She could have done whatever he asked, except this Jessica had made such an impact on her so that she could not promise her beloved that she will never think about Jessica again!

CHAPTER 10

Next morning, Shivangi went out to dive deep into the lives of plantation workers.

She surveyed many and found out more about their miserable life.

They were not happy with their working conditions. Many of them had to undergo long journey to reach their workplace. The workplaces lacked resting space and latrine facilities. The dust from the factories also created many health issues to the workers.

The workers were exhausted by the long and continuous working hours which lasted from 7:00 a.m. to 4:30 p.m. They asked the owners constantly to arrange it from 9:00 a.m. to 4:30 p.m., but in vain. Even though they were forced to work for a longer duration, only a low salary is given to them.

Actually, they are working in those tea plantations as they had no other choice. Many a times uprising would erupt, but they were suppressed by the local gundas who work for the factory owners.

They informed her about an uprising which took place three months before. It was led by the plantation workers under the leadership of Jessica. They demanded proper wage, drinking water, bonus, and gratuity. Gundas attacked some of the main protesters and killed one. The natives believe that they might be the one responsible for Jessica's death.

Shivangi tried to console them and asked them to hope for betterment.

"We have been hoping for a better life for a long time. How long do we have to wait? We are fed up with this horrible life. At times, we think of committing suicide. But then, our children will suffer. That is the only reason we are alive now," said Shanthimaya, a forty-six year old worker who had been working from the age of fourteen.

On her way back to the estate, she received a call from her project partner. She said that she will reach by 9:00 a.m. the next day.

CHAPTER 11

Steny Jacob, the Johny Lever of Bangalore Christian College. Shivangi's project partner.

She reached Kuttikkanm at 8:30 a.m., half an hour earlier than what she said.

Steny was innocent and talkative. Whenever she opened her mouth, stupidity overflowed. She couldn't help herself to stop it. She had a special ability to attract problems! She would invite problems and then struggle to flee from it but, she was funny and of pure heart.

Steny wasn't Shivangi's best friend, yet they had an invisible rapport. Even they didn't know how to explain it. Steny was the first one to hear many of Shivangi's secrets which she had never disclosed to anyone else. She didn't know what is the factor that made her disclose the secrets to Steny.

May be it was because of Steny's kindness and encouragement to go for her goals within a few months of knowing her, Steny made a special place in Shivangi's mind.

Steny was very tired after her journey. She slept till 4:30 p.m. after having breakfast. Shivangi thought not to disturb her and went for her meeting with Kannan alone.

She returned at 5 o'clock after having tea, she went for a walk around the estate with Steny.

"So, what did you find here? How's the life of workers here?" she asked.

"Pathetic, they are having a horrible life."

Shivangi then explained what she saw in Kuttikanam and what the workers told her, she also told her about the uprisings.

"Oh my God, it's so cruel to kill poor people who demand good living condition."

"Yeah, and they say that these gundas are responsible for Jessica's death too."

"Jessica? Who is that?"

Shivangi then told Steny about Jessica, her family, her social works and her death.

"Poor soul, what a nice girl she was," she exclaimed.

They went inside and sat in the main hall. Steny took a magazine and began skimming through the pages. Shivangi sat, looking deeply into Jessica's picture. She moved towards it and tried to light the diya again. And yes, it was a failure!

"What the hell is this?" she shouted.

"What the hell is what?" Steny asked without moving her eyes from the magazine.

"Why this diya doesn't hold the fire even for a minute? I have been trying for days! It is necessary to make her rest in peace, it is what we do for the dead people."

"Seems like she is not at all dead."

Even though Steny didn't mean what she said, her words had travelled deep in Shivangi's head. And it started everything!

CHAPTER 12

Shivangi kept pondering over Steny's words:

"Seems like she is not at all dead!"

"Maybe that is the reason the diya went off or was it because her soul is unhappy? But I have a strange feeling that she is alive. If it is so, where is she now? Is she being imprisoned by some kidnappers or is she just hiding herself?" she asked herself.

Later, she discussed it with Steny.

"Are you mad? You are not a Sherlock Holmes to go after crime investigation. We have a full-on project to think about," Steny said.

But Shivangi made an oath in her mind that she will do whatever she can to find the truth. She prayed to the Almighty to help her do this.

Next day, she set out early to meet Vinayan Mash.

"Morning, sir."

"Morning, Shivangi. How are you? Do you need my help?"

"Yes, sir," she replied.

"Do you want to know about the history of tea plantations or that of the first factory in Kuttikanam?"

"I want to know about Jessica."

He was rather amazed on hearing her reply.

"Jessica! Why do you want to know about her?"

"I don't know sir, I came to know about her from Chinnamma. She told me about her family and death. It would me really helpful if you could add something to it," she said and looked at him with hope.

"Jessica, she was an angel! Most efficient, brave and caring girl I have ever seen. She couldn't bare the pathetic plight of the workers and led a strike against the plantation owners. The cost she had to pay for this was her own life!" He said with a sigh.

"Are you sure that they are the ones behind her death?"

"Well, everyone says so. The police are also stating it. They are behind the gundas who disappeared after the death of Jessica."

"So everyone believes that she is dead."

"She is dead, dear Shivangi. Why you are having a doubt and what is the reason behind your immediate interest in Jessica?"

"I don't know how to explain it sir. You might feel that I have gone mad. I have a feeling that she is not dead," Shivangi said softly.

"What? But why? It's been three months and no information about Jessica," Mash told her.

"That is exactly what I am saying. No information doesn't mean that she is dead. Nor bloody belongings can prove it. What if she is alive now and is pleading for her rescue?"

Vinayan Mash stood confused.

"But the police say that she went missing four days after the workers uprising. The gundas who crushed the uprising has also disappeared."

"The gundas had killed another worker, I suppose. The workers told me so. That may be the reason for their hiding."

"Maybe if she is alive, the police could have found her by now," Mash said. "Sir, are you sure about that? You know about our police system. They won't succeed in finding truth at many times. Well, I don't blame them, mistakes can happen."

"You are right somewhere. But even if she is alive, what can we do? We are just ordinary people."

"Then who are all special ones? Everyone is ordinary. Only their intentions and activities make them special," she argued.

"Shivangi, I am in no place for an argument. This is what I know I'm sorry."

He walked away leaving Shivangi behind.

She then visited the police station. They informed what Vinayan Mash told her earlier. They also told her that they got information about the local gundas Raman and Kichu and now they are supposed to be in Bangalore. They will be off to Bangalore the very next day to catch them.

After few days, she heard that the gundas slipped from the hands of police and they returned empty handed.

Shivangi felt that nothing is on the right track. She decided to go Eranakulam and meet David. She decided to keep it a secret from her parents and Pulkit. She asked Steny to accompany her.

CHAPTER 13

Shivangi got David's phone number from Kannan. She didn't ask it from her uncle as he would question her.

David was indeed a busy man, so she took an appointment. He was happy as she was the family member of Divakar. She lied to him that she needed his life experiences about living in Kuttikanam and watching the worker's lives.

Shivangi and Steny reached the Le Meridian Hotel at Eranakulam around 4:30 p.m. David was waiting for them at the reception. He welcomed them.

He was tall, fair, and handsome, and still a bachelor. He reminded her of Emraan Hashmi!

Chinnamma had told her that he was just one year older than Jessica. Within a very short time, he had become a successful businessman.

Steny was fascinated to see him.

"Hey Shivangi, he is so hot, oh my God, I am gonna be in love with him," she whispered in Shivangi's ears.

"Shut up Steny."

"What happened? Is something wrong?" he asked on seeing their hush-hush.

"Oh, Steny was saying that it's too hot here," Shivangi replied with a smile.

They started with the beauty of Kuttikanam, the tea plantations, the workers, etc. At last, Shivangi drove the conversation to Jessica.

David burst out to tears on hearing the name 'Jessica'. Both Shivangi and Steny were spell-bound on seeing him cry. They tried to console him, but failed. They kept silent. After some time, he settled down.

"Jessica was a butterfly who brought the nectar of happiness in our family. My sweet little sister after my parents' death she was my only world! But..." he couldn't complete his words. He sobbed again.

"David , who do you think was responsible for her death?" Shivangi asked.

"I don't know Shivangi I just don't know whoever did it, they might be so cruel. How can they kill such a sweet person? During all these years, even I, her brother, could not even hurt her with a word and they, they killed her!"

"But how can you be so sure that she is dead?"

"She has been missing for the past three months," he replied

"And you got her belongings with blood spots in it. Does that mean that she is dead?" Shivangi stormed.

Steny pinched her to lower her voice and calm down. She asked why she is behaving so oddly with a man whom they have met for the first time. He looked puzzled by her reaction.

"I'm so sorry David, I know you are sad about your sister. Actually, I lied to you about the reason for my arrival. I wanted to enquire about Jessica," she said.

"Why is that?" asked a surprised David.

"I don't know what magic it is, I am having a strong feeling that Jessica is alive!"

His eyes popped out on hearing this.

"What! What are you saying? I think you are not normal. You girls drink? Maybe your drink has gotten into your head," he scorned.

"Please Mr. David, please hear me. We are not drunk. What if she is alive?"

"Look Shivangi, I have no time for your fantasies. Don't drag my poor sister into your funny stories. Let her rest in peace. Now, you may leave," he said and stood up.

"David, please hear me out," Shivangi pleaded.

He turned and said, "Please don't disturb me again."

Shivangi found no point in pleading to him. She walked towards the door along with Steny. She looked back and saw him staring at them.

"You could have behaved with some politeness. After all, you are talking to a man who had lost his three family members and is trying to manage his sorrows," Steny said.

"But he was not allowing me to discuss my doubts. His behaviour changed suddenly. Haven't you noticed it?"

"Stop it. You can't just misunderstand him. He is the one who is suffering a lot in his mind. It is common for such a person to react in this manner when he is hearing such rubbish things."

"Steny, it's not rubbish."

"Oh really! I think what David said was right. You are drunk."

"Steny..."

"Hush, not a single word. We are going back."

CHAPTER 14

Shivangi was searching for a book all over the room, one afternoon, when she got a couple of papers. It seemed to have been torn out from a diary.

"Feb 3 2017

It had happened, dear diary. Finally, it happened. He confessed to me his love!

Well, even though I began to feel something for him, I waited for him to come to me. After all, it would be shameful for a girl like 'me' to approach him, proclaiming my love!

I was preparing the report on the press meeting while he came to me. I thought it would be for some professional work. But it wasn't.

He handed me a paper by saying that correct it if something wrong. The content is as follows:

"Miss Jessica Mathew, it had been a long time I was trying to say something to you. I LOVE YOU JESSICA. I mean it. I took so long to tell this as I wanted to make sure that I am genuine about it."

I hid my smile and told him gravely that there is no mistake in it! He wondered why I was not responding as he wished. He thanked me for checking and left.

I laughed and laughed. I wanted to jump with joy! I wanted to run to him and kiss him! I was mad inside! He told me he loved me. I laughed and laughed. He was busy typing something in his laptop. I went to him and called him a duffer!

He was astonished and asked for the reason. I told him that I thought he could have walked straight to me, looked into my eyes and said, "I love you." I added that since he failed to do that, I will do it for him.

And then I said, "I love you Saquib!"

His facial expressions showed a mixture of surprise, happiness and shyness. I smiled and went out of the cabin. I looked back and saw him gaping. It was so cute to watch him stand like that. My poor little rabbit!"

The note ended.

"Now we have another character, her boyfriend Saquib," Shivangi told herself.

Jessica worked at 'Kerala Today' headquarters at Idukki. Kerala Today was a leading news channel in Kerala.

Shivangi reached her office and moved straight to the reception. A lady was sitting there.

"Can I meet Mr. Saquib?" asked Shivangi

"You mean Saquib Hussain?" she asked.

"Saquib Hussain? Yes, I think so."

"I'm afraid you can't. He is in a long leave."

"Oh no! It's an urgent matter. Do you have his contact number or address? Please help me out," she pleaded.

"Ma'am, I am sorry. I can't disclose his personal information to any stranger."

"Look, I am not a stranger. You remember Jessica Mathew, right?

I'm her cousin. I just wanted to deliver him some belongings of Jessica which she left out for him. I can't call him as I lost his number. At least give me his address so that I can reach out to him, please."

Shivangi lied as she had no other possible way to get to him.

"Oh, you are Jessica's cousin? What a kind person she was! She was like my sister. Please wait, I will get you his address," said the receptionist who fell for Shivangi's words.

The address was:-

Hussain Manzil

Pipeline Junction

Kattappana, Idukki

Shivangi reached his house by 4 o'clock. She rang the bell. No reply. She rang again. Then, a young man opened the door — Saquib.

CHAPTER 15

Saquib was a handsome calm man. She felt him to be the perfect person for Jessica. "They would make up a wonderful couple," she thought.

He seemed to be so tired. He might be having a fever or he might be disturbed because of Jessica's disappearance.

"You are Saquib Hussain, right?"

"Yes. But, who are you?" He seemed surprised.

"I'm Shivangi Manohar. You may not know me. But I know you. I know Jessica."

"You are Jessica's friend?"

"Well, sort of!"

"What does that mean?"

"Saquib, it is not a good thing that you are not inviting me inside," Shivangi smiled.

"Oh, I'm sorry. Please come in."

She entered the house. It was a neatly arranged place.

"Are you alone here?" she enquired.

"Yeah, my parents went to meet my sister."

"Good."

"Good? Why?"

"Oh, nothing."

"Actually, who are you?"

"I have revealed my identity a couple of minutes ago."

"You told me you are a 'sort of friend', what does that mean?"

"Saquib, I came to get some information of Jessica from you."

"And why do you want that?"

"To help her out!"

"To help her out?"

"Never mind. I am living in the estate which was owned by her earlier. I have read some of her writings and also heard a lot about her from the plantation workers. It made me arouse interest in her. I just wanted to know more about her."

"You came all the way just for that? It's not convincing."

"I am telling the truth, Saquib. I even went to meet David."

"David? Why are you so much interested in her?"

"Actually, I came here to complete a project on the plantation workers. Then I came to know about Jessica. I don't know why I am having a strange feeling that Jessica is alive."

"What?" He was stupefied.

"Don't think I am mad. You know, I left behind my project and now focussing only on Jessica. I haven't even informed my parents about it. I am serious. I want to help her out."

"First of all, we don't know whether she is alive. Even if it is so, why you are running behind all this? You haven't even met her before, right?"

"Yeah, but she and her story had taken away my peace of mind. I just can't focus on anything else."

She then told him about the repeated turning off of diya. He smiled and said,

"Shivangi, are you stupid? That may be the wind. How can you be so sure that Jessica is alive by looking at the diyas."

"Okay, leave the diyas. Her body is not yet found. How can you be that Jessica is dead?"

"The police says so!"

"Oh my God, what a law-fearing people we have! Is it necessary that whatever police says will have to be true?"

"Shivangi, they at least have some proofs to show. What do you have?"

"Faith. Hope. If you can, help me out. Otherwise, I won't trouble you again," she said and began to leave.

"No, please stop. I am sorry. I don't know what to say and how to behave nicely these days. I am on long leave as I can't face anybody. I don't want anybody's sympathy for my loss. I can't be in a place where Jessica is no more, I'm broken I'm helpless."

"Please don't be sorry. I know how it feels. Well, I'm glad that you are behaving a lot nicer than David."

"What did he say?"

"He drove me out of the hotel saying that I am drunk, while I said the same thing. Well, I don't blame him. It's not a normal thing that I said."

"Now I see, you very serious about this. I am with you. I am doing this for my Jessie. But what do we do now? Where to start?"

CHAPTER 16

"Saquib, just tell me how you met her and fell in love," Shivangi asked.

"Is this important?" he frowned.

"Yes, it is. Now, go on."

"I joined Kerala Today on the same day Jessica had joined. She was very professional and never went for stupid talks while at work. I had great respect for her. She just couldn't tolerate anyone suffering. I don't know when my respect turned into love."

"Does she have any professional enemies?"

"No, I don't think so. She was nice towards everyone. Nor she provoked celebrities or leaders, just like other journalists."

"So you are saying that the plantation owners were her only enemies?"

"Yes, I think so."

"But I don't. There is someone playing behind!"

Shivangi and Saquib exchanged their phone numbers and promised each other that they would call if they received some new information.

Shivangi had some shopping to do. So, when she reached the estate, it was night. There was no light. She remembered that Chinnamma asked for a half holiday. She must have gone. Steny too went to her cousin's home.

Shivangi took the keys to unlock but found the door open. Chinnamma, in the morning, had asked her to take the keys with her and told her that she will lock it using the spare keys. But the door was open.

"Is it a thief?" she thought with a horror.

She decided to call Kannan and the neighbours before stepping inside. What if the thief has deadly weapons!

She turned towards the gate and then THUD. Something hit on her head. She felt everything upside-down. She placed her hands on head and felt warm blood in her hands.

Shivangi turned to find a masked man in front of her. Even though she was bathed in fear, she decided not to surrender before him.

She tried to run away, but he caught her. He tried to choke her with his hands. Shivangi kicked and punched hard as she could to free herself from his fists. She couldn't even scream as his hands sealed her mouth. She felt that her end was near.

Suddenly, the silence was broken by a voice.

"Who is that?"

She saw a perplexed Chinnamma and her son. Her son Raju, without wasting anytime, took a log and ran towards them. The masked man might have understood that it was not safe. So he let her go and ran away.

"Shivi Mol, are you alright?" Chinnamma screamed while running towards her.

Shivangi felt darkness sweeping into her eyes. At the next moment, she fell unconscious.

When she opened her eyes, she found herself at the hospital. Chinnamma, Raju and Kannan were present. She was amused to see one person whom she never ever thought would be present — Saquib!

"Saquib! What are you doing here?"

Instead of Saquib, Chinnamma replied.

"Shivi Mol, after you got hospitalized, Saquib called to your phone. I explained what had happened. He reached here in no time."

Shivangi looked at him and he smiled.

"I am not rock hearted not to visit you when you are in this condition. Well, who do you think was that person?"

"A thief, may be. I don't know."

"Chechi, you don't have to worry. I have informed the police," Raju said. Actually, he came to drop Chinnamma to the estate during that night. And it made Shivangi get hold of her life!

"In all these years, no incidents like this happened before. I thought Kuttikanam was a place devoid of thieves. I was even proud of it. I don't think any of the old generation people would do that. It might be some new-gen boys," Chinnamma said angrily.

When Chinnamma, Kannan and Raju left for a while, Shivangi turned to Saquib.

"Hey, do you think this is normal?"

"What?" asked a confused Saquib.

"This attack."

"Yeah. Well, I don't know. What do you think?"

"Saquib , you are a bad actor. You can't hide your fear. It is very clear from your face."

"After you left from my home, I thought for a long time about what you said. I began to feel that something is wrong somewhere. I felt that you are right. So I called you and that is when Chinnamma told me everything."

Shivangi gave him a broad smile and he continued.

"You have been asking about Jessica to the natives as well, right? So what if this attack is also connected with Jessie? May be the one behind her disappearance feared that you will disclose him to the public and thus decided to finish you off!"

"It's exactly what I am thinking too," she said.

"I know that."

"But what will I do if he strikes again?"

"No, it won't happen. I have decided."

"Decided what?"

"To move to the estate with you!"

CHAPTER 17

Chinnamma was suspicious of Saquib in the beginning. She thought him to be Shivangi's boyfriend. But on knowing him for a couple of days, her approach softened. She certified him as sweet, nice, humble boy!

And to talk about Shivangi, she got someone to understand her completely. Within a few days, they had developed a strong bond. We can't blame Chinnamma for mistaking them to be lovers. Anyone who didn't know them well will think that they are bf-gf!

For her, Saquib was her 'bestest' friend. She never thought that one could become close friends within such a short period. The reason was that they thought about things at a same level. He understood her wild ideas and vice-versa. While talking , they understood that they shared common interests.

Steny was a bit mad at her as she feared she will fall in love with Saquib and will forget Pulkit. She even discussed it with Shivangi. But Shivangi was sure that he will remain as her best friend and brother. Oops,not as brother, as 'jiju'. Shivangi began considering Jessica as her elder sister.

Even though everyone asked her to inform her parents of the attack, she denied. Saquib threatened to tell the truth to Pulkit, but she pleaded to him and at last he dropped it.

One day, Shivangi was doing her evening walk with Saquib and Steny.

"Saquib, do your parents know about your relationship with Jessica?"

"Yeah Shivi, my parents, being orthodox, never wanted to accept her as their daughter-in-law."

"What if it was them who kidnapped her?" asked Steny without thinking.

Saquib frowned at her and Shivangi gestured her to stop talking rubbish.

"Sorry, I was kidding," Steny apologised after finding her joke go unsuccessful.

They continued their walk and reached the front porch when suddenly Steny noticed something in the sand.

"What is that?" she asked pointing to a shiny object.

Saquib bent and took it. It was a ring.

"Whose ring is this?" he asked.

"No idea," Shivangi replied

"Maybe, it is the ring of that masked man. Might have lost it during the struggle with you," Steny said.

"Maybe. Now, what do we do with it? Saquib, any idea?"

"Let us keep it Shivi. There is no point in giving it to the police. We can think of some way to get him."

CHAPTER 18

Shivangi literally forgot her purpose of arrival to Kuttikanam. She stopped collecting information required for her project work. Saquib advised her many times to give some time for it but she was too obsessed with Jessica.

Another incident happened at that time. Even though Shivangi forbade Kannan from telling about the attack to anyone, it slipped from his mouth. Divakar uncle came to know about it and through him, Shivangi's parents too.

"Shivi, you are not staying there for there for one more day. Leave that place and come to us," her mother said while she called.

"No. Amma, it's not possible. I won't leave this place unless and until I find Jessica."

"Are you mad? She is dead."

"No, she is not. The attack proves it!"

"Shivi, my dear, you are the only one we have. Please return for our sake.", Sulatha pleaded.

Her words placed Shivangi in a dilemma. Now, the time came for her to choose between her parents and Jessica.

On her right side was her parents, her amma and appa who did everything to comfort her, who couldn't bear even a slight pain creeping into her, who would not live without her.

And on her left side was Jessica, the sweet gentle angle who is now pleading for her life. It is true that she hadn't even met her before. But a strange rapport connected her with Jessica.

She decided to turn left.

"Amma, I know I am the only happiness you have. If I leave Kuttikanam now, I can't forgive myself. Jessica's face will haunt me for the rest of my life. I can't lead a peaceful life then. Don't worry, nothing will happen to me."

Sulatha was not ready to accept what Shivangi said but when Manohar compelled her, she allowed her to stay. Manohar had faith in every step Shivangi took. He believed that during this time also, his daughter is correct.

Pulkit called her after hearing it from Shivangi's parents. "Shivi, what the hell are you doing? Why didn't you tell me about this? What about the attack? Are you alright?"

"Wow, wow, wow! Man, one question at a time please."

"Why are you crazy behind that Jessica?"

"Pulkit, I'm only crazy behind the truth. I never told you because I know you would never allow me to do what I wanted. And about the attack proves that Jessica is alive."

"But what will you do if it happens again? You are all alone."

"No, I am not. Saquib is with me."

"Saquib? Who the hell is that?"

"He is Jessica's boyfriend."

"But, what is he doing in the estate? Well, he shouldn't be with you. He is Jessica's boyfriend, not yours. Ask him to return," continued an angry Pulkit.

"Hey, are you jealous? You fear that I will fall in love with him? You don't have faith in me?" Shivangi asked with a quiver in her voice.

"No, it is not that. I have faith in you. But think of what others will say? Do your parents know about him?"

"No, I have told everything except him staying with me. And about what others say, hell out with them. You don't have to listen to what others say. He is such a nice boy. He won't trouble me in any manner."

"Are you saying that he is nicer than me?"

"Pulkit..."

"Okay, Okay. I am coming to you."

"No, you are not coming and that is final. Saquib will protect me in case of any further attacks and he WILL NOT FALL IN LOVE with me," Shivangi said angrily.

"Shivi, it's not my doubts. It's my concern. I can't leave you in trouble."

"I can't focus if you are here with me. You better complete your project work. Don't worry about me. I am not a little girl. Besides, Saquib is with me. We are more like a brother-sister. He cares a lot."

"Really!" Pulkit said sarcastically.

"Come on don't mock your 'brother-in-law!" she said while laughing

"Oh my God, you are persuading me badly. All I want is that you have to stay happy and healthy."

"And I can promise you that now, please don't come. It is not safe for you."

"Is it safe for you?"

"No, as a matter of fact. But I don't care a bit. The things are entirely different if you have a loved one near you while fighting a battle. You have to focus on the battle, make sure that he or she is not hurt and so on. It is really very difficult. Please don't come and make my battle easy!"

"My girl, you have placed me in a difficult situation. I'm a man and it prevents me from letting my girl out into danger."

"Pulkit, swear on my name that you won't come. I can't risk your life."

"And I can't risk yours."

"I will never ever talk to you if you come here?"

"Don't be so hard. I will not come. Now, is it okay?"

"Yes, it is."

"My devil, I love you so much. And don't trouble my brother-in –law!"

"I won't leave you Pulkit. I love you."

CHAPTER 19

"So my brother-in-law is afraid that I will fall for you," said Saquib while they were having tea.

"Oh no, no Saquib, he is not afraid of that. He is worried about what people will say."

"So that's it. I will tell you something if you promise that you won't fight with me."

"I will decide whether to fight or not after hearing what you want to say. Now tell me."

"Shivi, I am returning to my home. I can't bear people mocking you just because of me," Saquib said in a low voice.

"Saquib, I'm gonna kill you if you dare to step out of this estate, I don't care what people say. And, you have promised me that you will protect me from further attacks, what will I do if someone hurts me after you leave this place?"

"But, Shivi..."

"No. You are staying and that's final," she said firmly.

"Guys, take a look at this I got it from my room while I was cleaning the cupboard."

Saquib and Shivangi turned and found Steny with a piece of paper in her hand. They took the paper and began reading it. It was a page from Jessica's diary.

"May 17, 2017

I don't know why David is behaving so wildly. Today he fought with papa when he declared that the estate will pass onto me after his death. He argued that the tradition states that the property has to be given to the son, not the daughter.

I never wanted any assets, especially this estate. So I asked dad to get it registered to David. But he was firm in his decision.

David, after a long round of argument, left home and hasn't returned yet. I pleaded him not to go, but he doesn't stop. I wonder where he is now?"

After reading, Saquib looked at Shivangi. She knew what was going through his mind.

"Is it David..."

"I don't know. We needed some more evidence to be sure."

"I knew it, I knew it. It was evident from his face that he is a criminal. I understood it from our first meeting," cried Steny.

"Oh really! I am afraid that you didn't say anything about him except that he is hot," Shivangi said with a stern look on her.

"But I had it in my mind," Steny said and retreated to her room.

"So, what are we supposed to do now, Saquib?"

"We will go and meet him at Ernakulam. I know his house."

"And are we gonna tell him that we suspect him for Jessica's disappearance?" she asked in a funny way.

"Yes."

"Nice joke. Now answer me clearly."

"I am not joking. That is exactly what we are gonna say. I want to see his reaction."

"You will get us killed, Saquib. I think it is not a good idea."

"Why are you afraid of him? Is it because of his behaviour on that night?"

"Well, yes. He was really mad."

"Maybe, that is because of his guilt."

"Will he do this to his sister?"

"Shivi, we hear of mother killing her child, son killing father and so on. It can happen."

"Are you sure that you want us to go and meet him?"

"Yes. Tomorrow."

Shivangi and Saquib reached David's home next morning and found it locked. They waited till evening but no sign of David. Even the watchman had no idea where he went.

They decided to leave with a heavy heart.

CHAPTER 20

Shivangi felt very sad as they missed David, even though she resisted Saquib's idea of meeting David.

And about Saquib, he was totally irritated. He shouted at them, even for small things throughout the following days.

Shivangi felt helpless. She didn't know what to do further. "How to make sure that David is behind all these happenings?" this thought prevailed in her mind.

She found two family photos of Jessica, one with her parents and the other with David. Chinnamma, on seeing her holding the photos, said that they were captured two days before Mr and Mrs Mathews' death. Their last family photo!

Shivangi kept staring at David. "Is he the one?" She repeated it continuously as if she was chanting a mantra.

"It is so beautiful."

She was suddenly startled by Steny's words. She found her wearing the ring that they found at the porch few days before. The attacker's ring.

"Steny, what are you doing? It is an evidence. Put that aside. Keep it safe."

"Don't worry. It is safe in my hands. Whose pictures are you holding?" she asked white she got hold of the family photos.

"I think this ring is very common among the people of Kuttikanam. Look, even David has one."

Shivangi was awestricken. She snatched it from Steny and looked closely. A shiver ran through her spines.

"Steny, fetch Saquib. Hurry!"

After she left. Shivangi sank into the sofa. "It's him! He is the one. He attacked me as I found the truth," she told herself.

"What happened? Why did you call me?" Saquib came and asked.

She looked at him and said nothing. She showed him the ring and pointed to the one David was wearing in the photo.

Saquib stood there, without uttering a single word.

"What now?" she asked slowly.

"I will kill him!"

"You won't. You can't. The court will punish him, not you. Our primary concern is how to find Jessica."

"But..."

"Control your anger, Saquib. I know how you feel. But you have to gain control over your emotions. It is gonna be tough game."

"Okay. I think we have to tell this to someone."

"Who?"

"ACP Ajitabh. He is a friend of mine. It would be helpful if we have someone like him with us. We can discuss with him what to do further."

They went to meet Ajitabh, that evening. They were careful to arrange the meeting at his home, not at the police station. They explained everything, from the beginning till the end.

"This is a very serious case. But will it assume that Jessica is alive?"

"Yes, sir. David's reaction when I told him about my doubt proves it," said Shivangi.

"But it can be because of his irritation at your search for Jessica," Ajitabh pointed out. "Well, it can be," Shivangi after saying this, looked to Saquib's face and found it dull. She held his hand tightly and said, "We can hope for the best. She is alive, my mind says so." He smiled.

"You don't have to worry. I am on it. And we will find out the truth," Ajitabh assured.

CHAPTER 21

Everything happened so fast. Ajitabh went to meet David in order to have an informal talk on Jessica's issue. Even Ajitabh felt that something was misplaced. He couldn't do anything legally since he did not have any solid evidence stating that he was the one behind Jessica's missing. But he could not be let loose as he could escape on learning that they are behind him.

So Ajitabh decided to arrest him for attacking Shivangi. Shivangi learnt about David's arrest through Saquib.

"Did they question him? What did Ajitabh say about it?" she asked.

"He is repeating over and over that he didn't do anything."

"Oh, all criminals say that often!"

"Can we see him? Will you please talk to Ajitabh about it?"

"I will do that Shivi. But why?"

"I just want to talk to him."

Ajitabh arranged their meeting with David next day evening. Shivangi's heart pounded as she neared to the police station.

David was staring at the blank wall when they went to see him. He saw them coming, but did not move. Shivangi called out to him.

"David, do you remember me?" she asked.

"You are that psycho girl, living in my estate now," he replied angrily. "I do not have amnesia. Now why have you come here? I know you are the one responsible for my present condition."

"If you didn't do anything, then why are you scared? Why are you behaving so madly at me? Why did you attack me?"

"How can you be so sure that I attacked you?"

"Your ring betrayed you,"

"Which ring?"

"This one," she said while point to his ring in her hand.

"The brilliant Shivangi suspected me just because of a ring. Poor, very poor! That was not at all intelligent. You know something, I lost my ring one month ago. There are many people with this kind of ring, not just me. And about my behaviour, this is me! I do not know to behave like the gentleman in your concept. It does not show that I am a criminal. It is true that I quarrelled with my sister for the estate's ownership, but it doesn't mean that I killed her for it."

"So you didn't kill her, right? Fine. Tell me where you kept her, hidden from everyone?"

"Shivangi, can you stop being a total jerk. I can assure you that I don't know anything. I did not kill her. I did not hide her. After all, she is my sister. You just can't make me guilty by just looking at a ring."

"David had a point. What if someone else is the actual convict?" she told herself.

When she raised this doubt to Saquib, he became angry and said, "Don't be a moron. Why are you thinking unnecessary things on hearing his words? Born criminals will say such things to confuse us. Now don't muddle up your head further. Let us pray and hope that he will tell the truth fast so that we can get our Jessica back."

Even though Saquib said so, she couldn't just erase it from her mind. This was Shivangi. She will catch anything that is thrown towards her and will continue to work on it till she gets a satisfying answer.

So now, she began working on the ball of doubt thrown to her by David.

CHAPTER 22

Three weeks had passed. Even though her project was not having any improvement, a lot of incidents had happened during the time, including David's arrest.

He had been presented to the court and the court lent the custody to the police for further investigation.

Saquib was in immense joy. It wasn't because of David's arrest; it was because soon he would be meeting his lady love Jessica. He had faith that the police would force him to reveal where Jessica was hidden.

Shivangi lost her peace of mind once again. A thought occurred to her that David is not guilty. She feared to disclose it to Saquib. He could storm out on hearing her.

Almost whole of Kuttikanam came to know about David's arrest. While some were happy to hear that Jessica is alive and will be found soon, others were shocked to hear about the cruelty of David. Some even began to say that David is the one behind the accident of his parents.

Chinnamma too came to know about it. She asked Shivangi whether she knew it before.

"To tell the fact, Saquib and I made him to go to jail."

"What?"

"Yes. We doubted that he is behind the disappearance of Jessica."

"Are you sure he is the one?"

To this question, silence was her reply.

"He was a bad boy from childhood," said Chinnamma.

"Who? David?"

"Who else. He was a mad child indeed. There is no end to the cruelty he had done. He would catch birds and will peel off their skin even when they are alive, when he was only fifteen years old."

"What? Are you serious?" asked a shocked Shivangi.

"Yes, of course. The list doesn't end here. Once I saw him writing something with the blood of the bird he had killed, in some papers."

"Writing with blood? What did he write?"

"I wasn't sure what it was. There was a lot of sings and symbols. He did many more things that would make any man unconscious. I have not enough guts to disclose it to you. I think he was doing some black magic."

"Black magic? David!"

Now Shivangi got another clue to hang about...

CHAPTER 23

Shivangi knew the place where she had to go. She reached Vinayan Mash's home and was disappointed to see his gate closed.

But she was fortunate enough to meet him on her way.

"Vinayan Mash, oh my God. Do you know how relieved I am to see you?"

He was rather amused to see her reaction. Her face was sparkling with immense happiness.

"It is nice to meet you Shivangi. But, why are you so happy on seeing me?"

"I just wanted to know something."

"Before that, kindly accept my apology."

"Apology, for what?"

"Shivangi, I thought you to be mad at the beginning, spending your valuable time on silly unrealistic things. But you proved me wrong. You are such a brilliant, compassionate and hard-working girl. You did it all alone. You found the culprit. And now, within a few more days, we will be able to see our Jessica."

"Sir, what did you feel when you came to know about David being the culprit?"

"I was shocked on hearing that he is the one behind all these incidents. I couldn't believe he could do such an activity in his life. He was such a nice boy in his younger days."

"Nice boy? Was he a nice boy in his young age, especially during teenage time?"

"Yes, of course."

"Are you sure?"

"Yes, I am. What happened Shivangi? Is there a problem?" asked a confused Vinayan Mash.

"How come you are so sure?"

"He came to my house for tuition class after his school hours during his school days. Such a bright student he was and also very responsible and disciplined. I heard about the fight regarding the estate's ownership. But will that make him do harmful things to his sister? I can't relate with it since I know for a long time."

"Sir, you said that he was a boy with brilliant behaviour in his teenage. But I heard something else about him?"

"Something?"

"Yes. That he was ... addicted to ... black magic during his younger days," Shivangi completed her sentence with great difficulty.

"What the hell!"

She was taken aback by the sudden and loud reaction from Vinayan Mash.

"Black magic? Who told you this rubbish? He may be guilty for Jessica's kidnapping. But that doesn't mean you can say whatever you want about him. Till twenty three years, I knew him well. And I can assure you that whatever you said was complete nonsense. From where did you hear this lie?"

"Oh, it's just... I heard this from a group of women," She lied as she didn't want to disclose Chinnamma's speech to him.

"Never believe what everyone says. David was not doing any black magic and that is the truth."

"Thank you so much sir. You don't know how you helped me today."

"I don't know what is going in your mind now. Whatever it is, I am sure that it will be for everyone's good. I believe you. May you succeed in your efforts, my child."

Shivangi felt an uplift in her mind. She bent down and touched his feet for his blessings.

Oh her way back to the estate, only one question was banging in her head – "Why did Chinnamma say such terrible lie about David?"

CHAPTER 24

By the time she reached the estate, Saquib was waiting eagerly for her.

"Where have you been? And didn't you take your phone with you? Pulkit has called. He was frustrated."

"Frustrated ? Why?" asked Shivangi.

"He complained to me that you are not giving him any time like you used to be. It is a true fact Shivangi. Tell me when did you call him last?"

"Well, I..."

"Shivangi, you are my best friend. You are more like a sister to me. And I can't let anything happen to you. I can't let your personal life affected while you are in a run behind finding Jessica. People will hold me responsible for it and I can't bare that."

"No one will say anything. As long as I know the real Saquib, don't open up your ears for others."

"And about Pulkit?"

"You said the answer to your question earlier. He is frustrated. He is frustrated as he can't come and help me."

"Shivangi, call him. Talk to him. It can soothe him. Go now. Take your phone."

Shivangi tried him four times, but he didn't pick up her call. She felt a heaviness in her mind. Finally, he answered her call.

"Hello, Pulkit?"

"What?" She was surprised to hear his arrogant tone. He had never ever used that tone to speak to her even if they are in a fight.

"Pulkit, I am so sorry. I know I am the guilty person. You can blame me. Please don't..."

"I am happy to hear that you didn't forget me," he said without changing his tone.

"Pulkit, please try to understand. Yes, it is my fault. But you know how I will be when I am engaged wholly in something."

"I know that. But this one is so different. First of all, you are engaged in a case that is completely dangerous. Okay, you succeeded in finding the criminal. Now answer my question. Why are you reluctant to call me even after you have solved the case? Is it because you are too comfortable with your so-called brother Saquib?"

Pulkit!" she screamed through the phone. She hadn't expected such kind of reaction from Pulkit. She wondered what happened to him. She felt that even though it was her fault that she didn't call him, she wished he could understand her a bit more and he couldn't have told her such things about Saquib. She tried to control her anger and continued,

"Look Pulkit, I told you several times I am the faulty person. The only one. There are three things that I want to inform you. First, Saquib has nothing to do with it. Do you remember that

I frequently told you about my wish of having a big brother. I got one now and he is Saquib! I have told you this before. I don't know what made you drag him into it again. I can't bare anyone blaming him for things that he never intended to do.

Second, you asked me that why I am ignoring you even after I solved the case. You are absolutely wrong, my dear. Even I thought I solved it. But I was wrong.

And the third thing, I LOVE YOU. Whatever happens, you are the only man in my life. Keep that in your mind."

There was a long silence. Then he spoke up.

"I am very sorry, Shivangi. I was mad. I don't know which devil worked on my mind. I'm sorry for what I have said. Please forgive me. And I love you too. I was dying to hear your voice. Now, don't worry about me. Whether you call me or not, I know how much you love me. You don't have to prove it by calling and talking to me. I was being a stupid man. I will try to finish my work here and will come to you. Till then you have to focus on the case and get it done rightly. When I get there, I want Jessica to receive me along with you. Take care Shivi, and love you."

"Love you Pulkit. Bye."

She stood there for some time. She then turned and was surprised to find Saquib standing there, with tears in his eyes. He ran towards her, hugged her tightly and began sobbing. Shivangi was flabbergasted by his action.

"Oh my god, is that you Saquib or a ghost of some ten year old child that got into your body?"

He didn't reply and continued crying.

"Hello? Can you tell me why are you crying?"

"I heard your conversation with Pulkit. I never thought you cared that much for me."

On hearing this Shivangi felt like laughing. She burst out.

"Oh my God, you are a silly boy. Was that the reason behind all these crying? I have never seen such an emotional boy ever in my life."

A faint smile appeared on his face.

"Saquib, you are my brother. I will fight with everyone who would try to disgrace you. I mean it!"

One drop of tear escaped from his left eye.

"Now, no more crying. If anyone sees you crying like this, it is a shame. Now stop this."

"Yes, I will." He rubbed his eyes. Suddenly, he remembered something.

"Shivi, why you told him that the case is not solved? What happened? Did I miss something?"

She sighed and looked at him.

CHAPTER 25

"Saquib, I think we are wrong."

"About what?"

"David. I think David is innocent."

"Shivi, we had discussed this before. You can't believe his words."

"It's not his words Saquib. It's some others'."

"Others'? Who?"

"Chinnamma told me that he was addicted to black magic in his teenage days. But Vinayan Mash completely rejects that. He even says that he was the most wonderful boy he had ever met during those days."

"So?"

"Why would Chinnamma lie to me?"

"I don't know. To give some more effect to David's story, maybe. People actually do that, you know."

"Yes, I know. But I thought Chinnamma was very different. And that she could not have gossiped."

"It might be true that David was good boy in his childhood days. But it cannot prove that he is not guilty now."

"But…"

"Shivi, enough of this. Let us pray to God to make him reveal soon where he is keeping Jessica."

She felt no point in provoking him further. She went to her room.

She sat by the window and stared outside, thinking how so many incidents happened in a swish. Nowadays she was not even thinking about her project. Her life had become a serious play. To say in Pulkit's words, the old Alia Bhatt had now become the Vidya Balan of *Kahaani*.

She felt her life curling up with new dues and excitement. Even now, she didn't know why she was so close to Jessica, without even seeing her.

"Maybe, she was my sister in the previous life!" she told herself.

Her mind wandered again. She recalled her life at Kuttikanam, from the very first day till that evening. She again got struck at what Chinnamma had said.

"Well, that was a very bad rumour. Black magic! It is not a common type of gossip," she thought.

That night, she decided to do some paper work of her project. She couldn't neglect it. Steny also sat with her, but was reluctant to do anything because of her laziness.

"I'm so bored. I can't do it anymore," she said.

"Slacker. You were resting during the whole day and still you can't concentrate on your work? Very bad!"

"Who told you I was resting?" Steny scorned.

"Then what were you doing?"

"I was reading," she said with a victorious smile.

"Reading? Really? I didn't expect that from you. Okay, which book?"

"It wasn't really a printed book. It was a hand-written manuscript on black magic."

Shivangi's eyes widened on hearing it.

"Manuscript on black magic?"

"Yes."

"From where did you get that?"

CHAPTER 26

CHAPTER 26

Saquib interrupted.

"It might be David's. I think Chinnamma is not gossiping. He must be the one practising black magic. The manuscript would be the one left behind by him."

"I got it from Chinnamma's room. It was lying on her table," Steny said.

"Chinnamma's table!" Shivangi and Saquib said in unison.

Chinnamma had gone to her home that morning after taking permission from Shivangi. Even though she is a servant, she had her own room in the estate.

"But tell me why did you go to her room?" Saquib asked.

"To get my pain-relief spray which I had given to her yesterday. But she was not there."

"She asked my permission to go to her house."

"Yeah, I remember. I found this book lying on her table and took it for reading."

"A Malayalam book?"

"I read it with the help of Google translator. It is full of the practices done by people doing Sathan Seva?"

"Sathan seva?"

"Yes, practices done to please Sathan, the devil."

"But why is it with her?" asked a confused Shivangi.

"She might have got it from David's room many years back. She might have kept it with her," Saquib explained his theory.

"But Steny said that it was 'on' the table. This proves that she was reading it currently."

Saquib shrugged. "Maybe she decided to see what was in it."

"After all these years?" Shivangi frowned.

"Yeah."

"Okay, I believe it for now, Saquib."

"Shivi, what about this book?" Steny asked pointing to the manuscript.

"Leave it in Chinnamma's room," Saquib said.

"No, I'll take it."

"Shivi, why do you want that?" Saquib scorned.

"Oh, I just wanna take a look at it."

"Well, it is horrible," warned Steny.

They continued their paperwork till 10 o'clock. After that, Steny went to sleep. But Shivangi didn't feel like sleeping. So she decided to take a look at the manuscript. It was not a difficult task for her as she knew the Malayalam alphabets well. Manohar had taught her to read and write in Malayalam.

"BLACK MAGIC – It is done to help you gain something.

It can be used for different purposes:-

1) To bound someone in place. If someone is harming you and you wish to stop them.
2) To achieve immortality or improve your health.
3) To communicate with the dead.
4) To cast love spells.

Rituals:-

A site is chosen for casting the curse or spell. A circle is drawn on the casting site and a pentacle is drawn inside the circle. This is called circle of power.

Candles, herbs, crystals and charms are employed to help draw out the spirit. Word of power is repeated 3 times.

Spirits will have a harder time visiting a location that is populated by a lot of people, so choose a place in the woods or another area not frequently visited.

- Step into the circle of power. Gather concentration. Do not get distracted.
- Recite the words of power associated with your desired spell.
- Use black clothes while doing the ceremony.
- Poppet should be made from natural materials. Fill the poppet with earth and hair

or nail clippings from the person whom you want to hex.

- Let the candles burn down. Once they have burned completely, the hex has been cast."

Shivangi dozed off before completing the manuscript.

CHAPTER 27

Jessica was tied to a tree. There were candles around the tree. Drum beats could be heard clearly. Someone in a black hood moved slowly towards her. He had a knife in his hand. He raised it and...

"Noooooo..."

Shivangi woke up with a start. She felt relieved to find that it was only a dream.

"Shivi, are you alright?" they called out.

"Yes, I am. It was only a dream; a bad one. Don't worry," she replied.

Now, it was difficult for her to go back to sleep. The Goddess of sleep seemed to be angry with her. So, she decided to read the manuscript completely.It was nearly 8 o'clock in the morning when she stepped out of her room. Her eyes were red due to lack of sleep.

Saquib was drinking coffee at that time. She went and sat beside him. He stopped drinking as he looked at her face.

"What the hell Shivi!" he cried in surprise.

"What?"

"Look at your eyes!"

"My eyes?"

"It is bright red. Didn't you sleep well?"

"As a matter of fact, no. That nightmare took away my sleep."

"Was that so bad?"

"Yup."

"What was it about?"

Shivangi thought for a while whether to tell him or not. Then she continued.

"I saw someone with a black hood. He was going to kill Jessica with a knife. Suddenly I woke up," she said in a single breath.

She saw horror sweeping into Saquib's face.

"Saquib, come on. It's just a dream."

"Yeah, just a dream," he repeated as if he was a school boy repeating the alphabets after his teacher.

"Hey guys, good morning."

They looked and saw Steny. It seemed that she was going out.

"I am going out. Will be back in the evening."

"Out? Where?" Shivangi asked.

"I'm gonna meet the plantation workers. I also want to hear their stories."

It was then that she noticed Shivangi's face.

"Are you not well?"

"Oh, it's just lack of good sleep."

"Then take rest and stay here."

"But you don't know the place very well Steny. You could get lost in this place,"

"C'mon Shivi , I am not a child. Now, let me go,"

"Okay Bye. Work well Steny," she said sarcastically.

Steny walked abruptly out of the house.

"My poor Johny Lever," Shivangi said with a smile.

CHAPTER 28

It's been half past five. Steny hasn't returned yet. Shivangi tried to call her, but she wasn't picking up her call. A strange thought crept into her mind. Without wasting anytime, she fetched Saquib and both went out, looking for Steny.

They didn't have any clue, where to search her. They went to Naran's factory and asked the workers about her. They told that they had seen her in the morning, but didn't know where she went after that.

Both Saquib and Shivangi were so frightened. They didn't know what to do next. She cursed herself for letting Steny go alone.

Suddenly, her phone beeped. She took it and was relieved. It was Steny's call!

"Steny tell me, where are you now?"

"Shivi, you know something? I am a fool."

"Oh, I know that. But where are you?"

"I decided to get back after seeing the plantation workers. But then, an idea struck my mind. I decided to experience the forests of Kuttikanam..."

"And?"

"I am trapped. I don't remember the way I came here. The forest is so confusing. I can't get out. Please help me Shivi."

"Stay where you are. I'm coming," Shivangi said wiping sweat buds from her forehead.

"What happened? Where is she?" Saquib asked.

"In the forest!"

"What?"

"Yeah. Come, let's get her,"

They headed towards the forest-stretch that looked like a huge green crocodile. The thing that troubled them was where to start?

They entered the forest from a way which they chose by singing 'inky pinky ponkey'! The light was fading away. The darkness began creeping in along with fear. What Shivangi and Saquib felt in their minds cannot be expressed in words. Time went by. They walked on and on, but could not find Steny.

After walking for about half an hour, they stopped. It wasn't because they were tired. It was because they heard a sound. Although they couldn't distinguish it as that of a human or an animal, they decided to walk towards the direction of the sound.

They moved slowly as they were not sure of the sound, whether it was produced by a human. It came from the area behind long cluster of bushes. They peeped through them.

What they saw there was the most unexpected thing they could think of! And the person whom they saw there was the last person they could think of to find at that place!

Standing there, dressed in black saree and blouse was none other than Chinnamma! Her hair was untied and a huge red thilak was on her forehead. Two elderly men were standing beside her.

Shivangi and Saquib looked at each other's face, gaping. They saw a man taking out a stick and drawing a pentacle within a circle.

"The circle of power!," Shivangi told herself.

Then they lit candles around it.

According to Shivangi, Chinnamma looked like a horrible witch in her attire. She wasn't the one whom they knew before.

She felt her to be the mad old witch from the tale of Snow White.

Slowly, Chinnamma moved to the centre of the circle. She was holding a poppet in her hands. She closed her eyes and began chanting the spell.

"I bind your feet from bringing you to harm me. I bind your hands from reaching out to harm me. I bind your mouth from spreading tales to harm me. I bind your mind from sending energy to harm me."

Saying this, she covered the poppet with a black cloth. She then placed it in the centre and stepped out. Then, all of them began crying out loud, 'Hail Sathan, hail Sathan, hail Sathan!'

With this, they left the place.

Shivangi's felt a chill running down her spine. She held Saquib's hand tightly. When they became sure of the group's retreat, they decided to move.

Shivangi's face was stiffened as she recalled what had just happened. Chinnamma and black magic?

Even now, she found it difficult to believe. Chinnamma doing a binding spell? How long had she been doing this? Questions filled in her mind.

Now, it was complete darkness. Even though they had mobile phones, they feared to turn on the light.

Suddenly, she bumped into someone. Shivangi froze. She thought it to be someone from the group. She felt her end near.

"I knew you would come for me!"

It was none other than Steny!

CHAPTER 29

Next day, Shivangi, Saquib and Steny were having breakfast. None of them had spoken anything about the previous night. Steny didn't know what Shivangi and Saquib had seen in the forest.

Even though their minds were churning out with emotions, including shock, fear and confusion, Saquib and Shivangi did not disclose it.

Chinnamma hadn't returned yet. Shivangi felt her body shivering even at the thought of the events she had witnessed.

After breakfast, Shivangi was sitting in the front porch, while Saquib approached her.

"Shivi?"

"Yeah"

They both looked into each other's face, unable to utter a word. After a few minutes, Saquib spoke up.

"So, what do you think about the events we saw yesterday?"

"I'm shocked, Saquib. Terror covers me when I think of that. It isn't because I had watched a black magic ritual. It was because Chinnamma did that. How could she? She used to be a lovely person. It's hard for me to believe that all the sweetness she had delivered to us is a mere drama."

"Shivi, now I am having a feeling that David is innocent."

Are you saying that Chinnamma is guilty?"

"There is no evidence that Chinnamma is the one behind Jessica's disappearance. We had only seen her doing a ritual. But a strange feeling occurs to me that she is guilty."

"Me too!"

"What are we gonna do?"

"We have to investigate it, and no Ajitabh this time. No one should know about this, even Steny."

"What is the plan?"

"We have to keep a close watch on Chinnamma, her home and her surroundings."

"Shivi, are you serious? We are just two people."

"So what? Don't think about your weaknesses. Focus only on your strengths, and we are gonna find it out."

"But can you say why we are feeling all these doubts even when we have no evidence?"

"Saquib don't think too deep regarding it. God wants us to know the truth. He is opening up new ways for us to reach it. If someone thinks in a critical manner and join all the actions and words of Chinnamma together, one will surely suspect her. The problem is that nobody is resorting to such critical thinking. People will find it difficult to accept our theory. Actually, a 'Mandela Effect' is working here! We can provide proofs on our arguments. But what is more interesting is that people who oppose us can also provide proofs regarding their arguments. Even though truth lies only in one side, it will seem both sides are correct!"

"What about Jessica?"

"I don't know. What if the binding spell was performed to keep her immobile?"

"Shivi, how can we be sure that she is alive?"

"No idea. People will call us lunatics, will they? Going behind people without having proper evidence. But we can't just ignore the doubts that we have in our mind."

"Yes, that's true. And don't worry. We will find truth regarding Chinnamma and her connection with Jessica's case. She is in our "guilt list" unless and until we find anything that would prove her innocent, no matter what others may think."

They heard the gates open and looked around. It was Chinnamma.

CHAPTER 30

"Hi Shivi Mol. I am sorry for my late arrival. There was a bit of things to be done in my home," Chinnamma said.

"It's okay," Shivangi uttered with great difficulty. Smiling at them, Chinnamma walked inside.

"Now what?" Shivangi asked Saquib.

"Let us go to Chinnamma's house," he replied.

"And?"

"Let us look for clues."

"I think her son would be there."

"So what? I never meant to squeeze into the house and search silently. We will go to her house with her and will persuade her to allow you to look into each thing 'because of curiosity' ."

"Will that work?"

"I don't know!" he shrugged.

"Okay, let's try."

That evening, Shivangi approached Chinnamma and asked her with an innocence that she build up with a great effort.

"Chinnamma, I have been visiting the homes of a lot of workers here. When will I be able to come to your home? It would be a great loss if I don't visit your house."

"You are always welcome, Shivi Mol. You can come with me tomorrow."

"Thank you so much Chinnamma."

"I'm sorry for not inviting you before."

"Please, don't be sorry."

The next day, Shivangi, Saquib, and Steny went to Chinnamma's home along with her.

Her son was present when they reached the place. He welcomed them and invited them inside. Both Saquib's and Shivangi's eyes were working like that of a hawk, they were searching for clues. Shivangi could not focus on what others were saying and so did Saquib. Finally, her eyes got struck in a photo.

"Chinnamma, who is that man?" she asked pointing to a man in a photograph.

"Oh, it's Nakul, my elder son," she replied.

"Elder son! I thought you had only one son. You never talked about Nakul."

"Sorry for that. He is working in Kochi as an electrician. He is not here at the moment."

"Okay."

"Amma, make something for them. They are visiting here for the first time. You gotta make something special."

"Yes, I forgot. Please wait, I will make my favourite 'bajji' for you guys." Telling that she moved to the kitchen.

Shivangi got up to take a close look at the photos hanging in the wall. She stopped at the one which she pointed out earlier. Nakul seemed familiar to her. But she couldn't remember her meeting him. It felt strange.

And then, she froze, what gave her a chill was what she saw in his hand!

She tried hard to submerge the arising feelings. But she failed to do so. While Raju and Steny were conversing, Shivangi grabbed Saquib and went outside.

"What happened? Have you got something?"

"He did that!" she gasped.

"Who did what?"

"Nakul. He was the one behind the attack on me that night. The ring belongs to him."

"Are you sure?" said an amazed Saquib.

"I am damn sure."

"What are we gonna do now Shivi?"

"Let us go to Ajitabh now. We can't be late/"

What Shivangi didn't know was the fact that Saquib was not the only one hearing her!

CHAPTER 31

"We must not have waited this long," Nakul said.

"But we could not have done it earlier. It is not good for us to do the sacrifice before time," replied Chinnamma.

"But..."

"Whether a lamb or a human, sacrifice should not be done before time. And that's final."

<......................................>

Shivangi and Saquib went to meet Ajitabh after dropping Steny at the estate. After listening to them, his face turned red.

"Do you think this is child's play? The police department is not to dance according to your orders. David is here because of you two. Now you want Chinnamma too locked in Jail?" Ajitabh scorned.

"We want the guilty to be in prison," Shivangi said firmly.

"And how can you be so sure that she is guilty? Because of Nakul's ring? Well, one ring bought David behind the bars. Now you want another person in jail because of a ring. Are you so silly Shivangi? And you Saquib, are you nuts to get her to me?"

"But Ajitabh..."

"Please, I have work to do," saying that he got up.

Shivangi was filled with fury. She jumped and said, "I don't need your help. I will gather proof against her and I will find Jessica."

She then lashed out of the room.

<....................................>

Saquib and Shivangi, on the following days, kept a close watch on Chinnamma's house. After two days of watching, they spotted Nakul. Then they followed him like a shadow, to his workplace, friend's house, bar, etc. No use at all! They even started following Raju, even though they felt him to be innocent.

But something happened on the fifth day. On that day, Raju took a different path, which is not usually used by him. In fact, none of the people used that road, it seemed so!

<...............................>

A huge factory the road took them to it. It was an inactive rubber factory, the one which seemed without human touch for years.

Raju disappeared into the factory. Saquib and Shivangi decided not to go inside and decided to check it out on some other day, when Raju was not around.

<....................................>

Next morning, they went to explore the factory. It was indeed, in a remote place, far away from the town. Its rusty look gave an eerie feeling.

They reached the backyard of the factory and found a door through which Raju entered the previous day. Saquib and Shivangi found it locked. Saquib was not ready to give up. He took a rock and began hitting the lock harder. It wasn't doing any good but he doesn't stop. After hitting for about five minutes, the lock gave up.

The interior was dusty and dark. Spider webs hung like they were fitted for decoration. The smell was very awful. It was hard to breathe.

The door opened to a large hall. Even though it was not functioning, the machines weren't removed. It led to another hall full of trolleys. There were several small rooms at one side, five to say clearly.

They opened the first one. It was full of old rubber mats. The second one, the third one, and the fourth one too. When Shivangi placed her hand on the knob of fifth door. Saquib said, "Hey, leave it Shivi. It also will be of rubber mats."

"What harm can it do by just looking," saying so she opened the road.

"Oh God…" she cried.

There she was, tied to a chair, unconscious — JESSICA!

CHAPTER 32

Shivangi was standing in the garden. Cool breeze swept slowly through her hair. She closed her eyes and listened to it. She felt immense pleasure.

She thought about the incidents that took place since the last month. Her arrival to Kuttikanam, the query for Jessica, the quest of David, Chinnamma's secret, etc. ran into her mind. Even now, she didn't know how to express the strange rapport she felt towards Jessica.

"Shivi..."

She turned to find Jessica standing beside her.

"What happened?"

"Nothing Jessi Chechi."

"Well, there is a shocking news."

"Shocking news?"

"Yeah. Chinnamma's house got burned down."

"What! How?"

"Cause is not known. But from the present situation, we can assume that it is a suicide attempt. They have feared that they will get exposed."

"You are right. It's been only a day that you are free. Raju might have found out. Chinnamma too didn't come back. Did anyone survive the fire?"

"Alas! No. The police found three bodies. Might be Chinnamma, Nakul and Raju,"

"Hey girls, what's going on?"

"Nothing Saquib, just discussing about Chinnamma and the fire," replied Jessica.

"Just leave it. You are free and the bad got punished. Happy ending ! And stop discussing it over and over again."

"Okay. But it's hard for me to believe one thing. They kidnapped and kept me alive for three months for a sacrificial ceremony! It was so stupid of them to keep me alive for such a long time. Too hard to believe!

EPILOGUE I

The time has arrived for Shivangi to leave.

Saquib has explained everything to Ajitabh. He felt so ashamed of himself as he could not help them in the process. And of course, David was released.

David was so happy to see Jessica. He ran towards her and hugged her tightly. Tear rolled down his cheeks.

"You don't know Jessi how much happy I am right now," he said while sobbing.

"Me too David."

As promised earlier, Pulkit came to pick her. Shivangi jumped onto him out of joy. She was like a Koala bear clinging to a tree. After the initial expressions of happiness, she introduced him to everyone present there.

When the time to say goodbye approached, Saquib was crying like a four-year old child. Jessica and Shivangi tried hard to keep him quiet. He was such an emotional boy!

Then Jessica started speaking:

"Shivi, I don't know what to say. We do not have any blood relationship. Yet, you set aside all your work and focused only on finding me. It is impossible for one to give an explanation to your actions and thoughts. There was no need for you to look for me, but you did so. And because of that, I am here, standing before you, alive. Thank you Shivi."

"Please don't embarrass me by saying thank you," Shivangi said while trying to control her tears.

Once again saying goodbye to Jessica, Saquib, David, and Kannan; Shivangi, Pulkit, and Steny started their journey to Karnataka.

EPILOGUE

II

Vinayan Mash had just ended his conversation with some tourists when he saw Jessica.

"Oh Jessi Mol, finally you are here. You don't know what I am feeling now."

"It's good to see you, sir."

"Well, take rest for some days and don't wander here and there."

"No, sir. I am alright. Actually I am planning to restart my investigation regarding black market and illegal drug distribution to tourists, which I was doing before my kidnap."

"Oh, good. All the best!"

"Thank you, sir," saying that, she left.

He looked her till she disappeared behind his vision. Then he said to himself,

"God, why do you want me to do that again? And that fool Raju, he didn't kill her right away after I gave him the contract. He was so stupid to keep her alive for the sacrifice of his mother's bloody black magic ceremony. Fuck him. But this time, I won't fail. Jessica, there is no one to save you now. Dear Jessica, angel of death is waiting for you..."